SFLEP – Longman Secondary Engli

外教社 — 朗文中学英语分级阅读

新课标百科丛书

说梦

DREAMS

新课标

第 9 级

之十一

上海外语教育出版社

外教社 SHANGHAI FOREIGN LANGUAGE EDUCATION PRESS

Longman 朗文

KEN BEATTY

图书在版编目（CIP）数据

说梦=Dreams /（加）比尔蒂（Beatty, K.）著.

—上海：上海外语教育出版社，2006（2008重印）

（外教社—朗文中学英语分级阅读：新课标百科丛书）

ISBN 978-7-5446-0098-9

Ⅰ. 说… Ⅱ. 比… Ⅲ. 英语—阅读教学—中学—课外读物

Ⅳ. G634.413

中国版本图书馆CIP数据核字（2006）第051121号

图字：09-2003-188号

作　　者：Ken Beatty

出 版 人：庄智象（外教社）　吴天祝（朗文）

策划编辑：林心心　陈　骅（朗文）

责任编辑：刘　芯（外教社）　Laura Hepburn, Bobo Wong（朗文）

美术总监：孔繁生（朗文）

出版发行：上海外语教育出版社

（上海外国语大学内）　邮编：200083

电　　话：021-65425300（总机）

电子邮箱：bookinfo@sflep.com.cn

网　　址：http://www.sflep.com.cn　http://www.sflep.com

责任编辑：刘　芯

印　　刷：上海图宇印刷有限公司

经　　销：新华书店上海发行所

开　　本：889×1280　1/32　印张 2　字数 48 千字

版　　次：2006年7月第1版　2008年10月第2次印刷

印　　数：10 000 册

书　　号：ISBN 978-7-5446-0098-9 / G・0051

定　　价：6.00 元

出版说明

随着新《英语课程标准》（以下简称《新课标》）的颁布，中学英语教学改革推进到了一个新的阶段，对学生的知识面、交际能力、文化意识等方面的要求提到了新的高度。课外阅读不再是课堂教学可有可无的补充，而已成为英语学习不可或缺的部分。《新课标》对学生课外阅读在数量上作出了明确的规定，在培养目标上提出了一系列新的要求。为此，上海外语教育出版社与朗文合作编写了这套“外教社—朗文中学英语分级阅读：新课标百科丛书”。其目的是将《新课标》的教学理念贯彻到课外阅读当中，帮助学生达到《新课标》所提出的各项要求。

丛书的编写以《新课标》为指导，主要有以下特点：1. 在总体设计上，根据《新课标》分级编写，针对性强，充分满足各阶段中学生的阅读需求；2. 在选材上，突出个性化特征，根据不同年龄段学生的不同阅读兴趣，选择具有时代感、内容丰富的题材，帮助学生在完成《新课标》阅读任务的同时，扩大知识面，培养跨文化交流意识；3. 在难度的把握上，兼顾能力的提高和阅读兴趣及自信心的培养，为学生营造宽松的学习氛围；4. 在学习策略的指导上，根据《新课标》对各级的要求为每册书编写阅读技巧指南，引导学生养成良好的学习习惯；5. 在单元后的练习编排上，突出灵活性、开放性及参与性，将读、说、写等相结合，激发学生的想象力和创造力，帮助学生全面达到《新课标》的各项要求。

丛书共80册，分3、5、7、9四级，每级各20册。本丛书与“外教社·朗文小学英语分级阅读”一脉相承，是外教社与朗文合作推出的阅读精品。

作为以《新课标》为指导编写课外阅读的积极尝试，我们衷心希望广大读者能够多与我们联系、沟通，提出宝贵的意见和建议，协助我们精益求精，将丛书不断提高、完善。

上海外语教育出版社

Acknowledgements

We would like to thank the following for permission to reproduce photographs and artwork:

Pearson Education Asia Ltd; Lau Siu Yuen; Corbis; Corel; Dorling Kindersley; Wikipedia; A'Lelia Bundles/ Walker Family Collection/madamcjwalker.com.

In spite of numerous efforts, we have been unable to trace all copyright holders. We should like to apologise for the infringement of copyright so caused and will be happy to make appropriate arrangements at the first opportunity.

Contents

Do you know?

- What is REM sleep?
- Why are we paralysed at certain times during a night's sleep?
- Does everybody dream the same amount?
- Can unborn babies dream?
- What is a lucid dream?
- How did Hippocrates help diagnose his patients' illness?
- What can it mean when people dream of being chased?
- What does Carl Jung say about elephants in dreams?

Read this book and find the answers to these and other questions. Learn about your own and other people's dreams. You'll be amazed!

The Land of Dreams

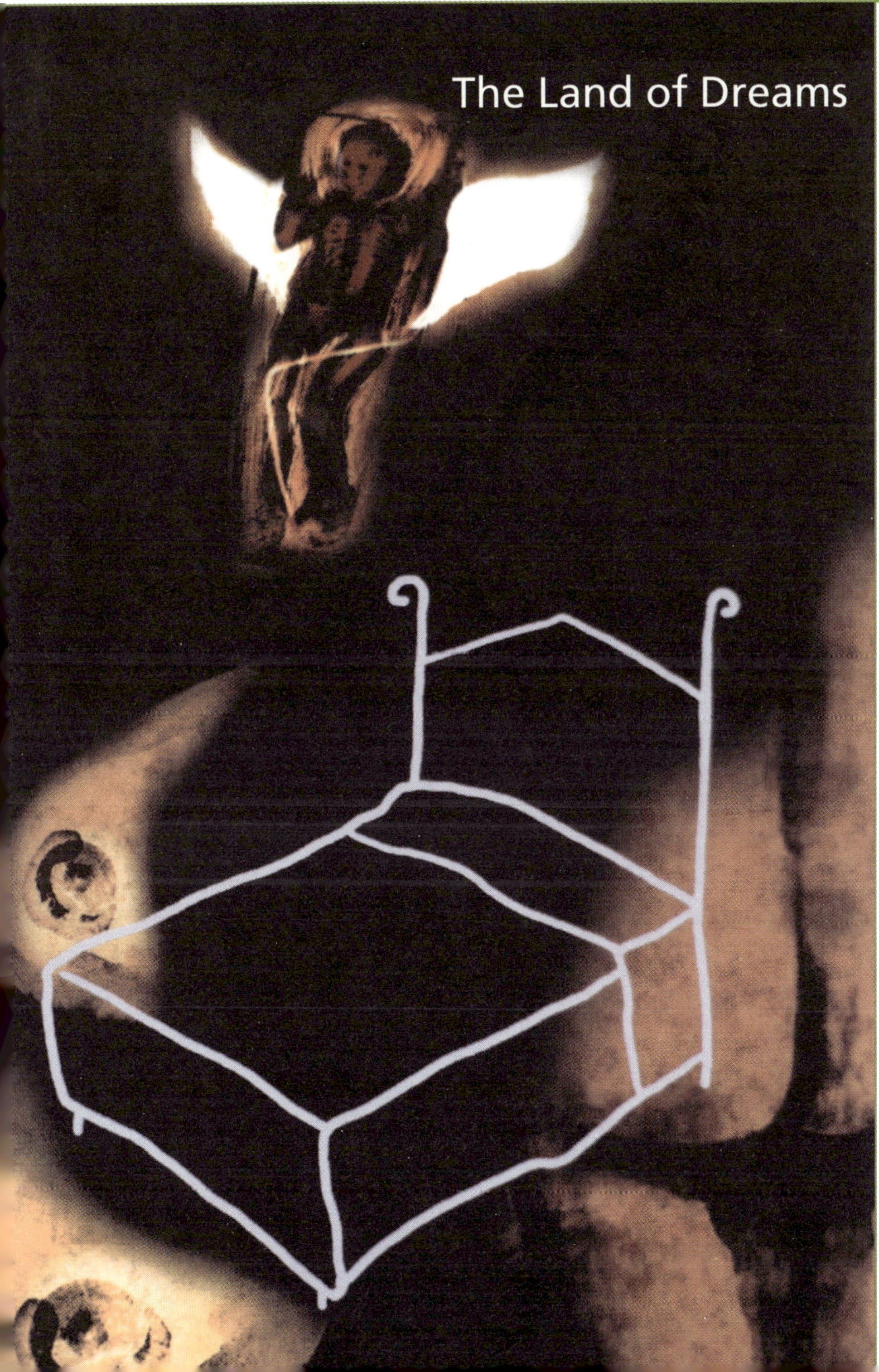

The Land of Dreams

Imagine there was a strange place where you were going to spend six years of your life. Would you be interested in knowing more about it? The fact is, you will spend about six years of your life in the land of dreams, but you have probably never thought much about why you go there, how you get there, or what you do there.

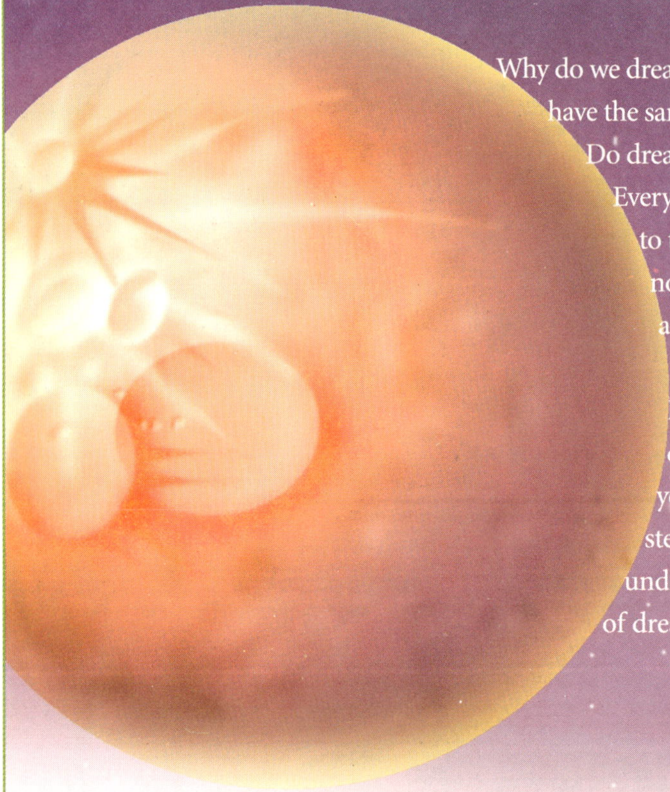

Why do we dream? Does everybody have the same types of dreams? Do dreams mean anything? Everyone of us has travelled to the land of dreams, but not many of us can answer these questions.

By thinking about the questions on page 5, you will take the first step towards a better understanding of the land of dreams.

What Do You Know about Your Dreams?

Answer these questions.

1. Are your dreams different every time or do they sometimes repeat?
2. Do you dream in colour, black and white, or a combination of the two?
3. In what language do you dream? Have you ever dreamt in a foreign language?
4. Which of the following have happened in your dreams? Tick the boxes.
   - ☐ a future event
   - ☐ being chased
   - ☐ losing your teeth
   - ☐ failing an exam
   - ☐ falling
   - ☐ flying
5. Are your dreams usually based on something you have recently seen, heard, or done?
6. Do you have nightmares? What are they usually about?
7. Are you always yourself in your dreams or are you sometimes someone else?
8. Do you think your dreams mean anything?

NOTES

combination / ˌkɒmbɪˈneɪʃən / 组合，结合

nightmare / ˈnaɪtmeəʳ / 恶梦

What kind of dreams are they?

Dreams are things that we see in our sleep, but we also call our hopes for the future 'dreams'. This book is about the dreams we have in our sleep. Which type of dream is each poem below talking about?

A

Dreams

Hold fast to dreams
For if dreams die
Life is a broken-winged bird
That cannot fly.

Hold fast to dreams
For when dreams go
Life is a barren field
Frozen with snow.

Langston Hughes

B

Dreams

I was a pretty butterfly
Floating high up in the sky
But then a bird came flying by
And ate me.

I woke and found I was not eaten
In fact, I simply had been dreaming.

Laura Hepburn

Answer: A – hopes for the future; B – dreams we have in our sleep

Sleeping and Dreaming

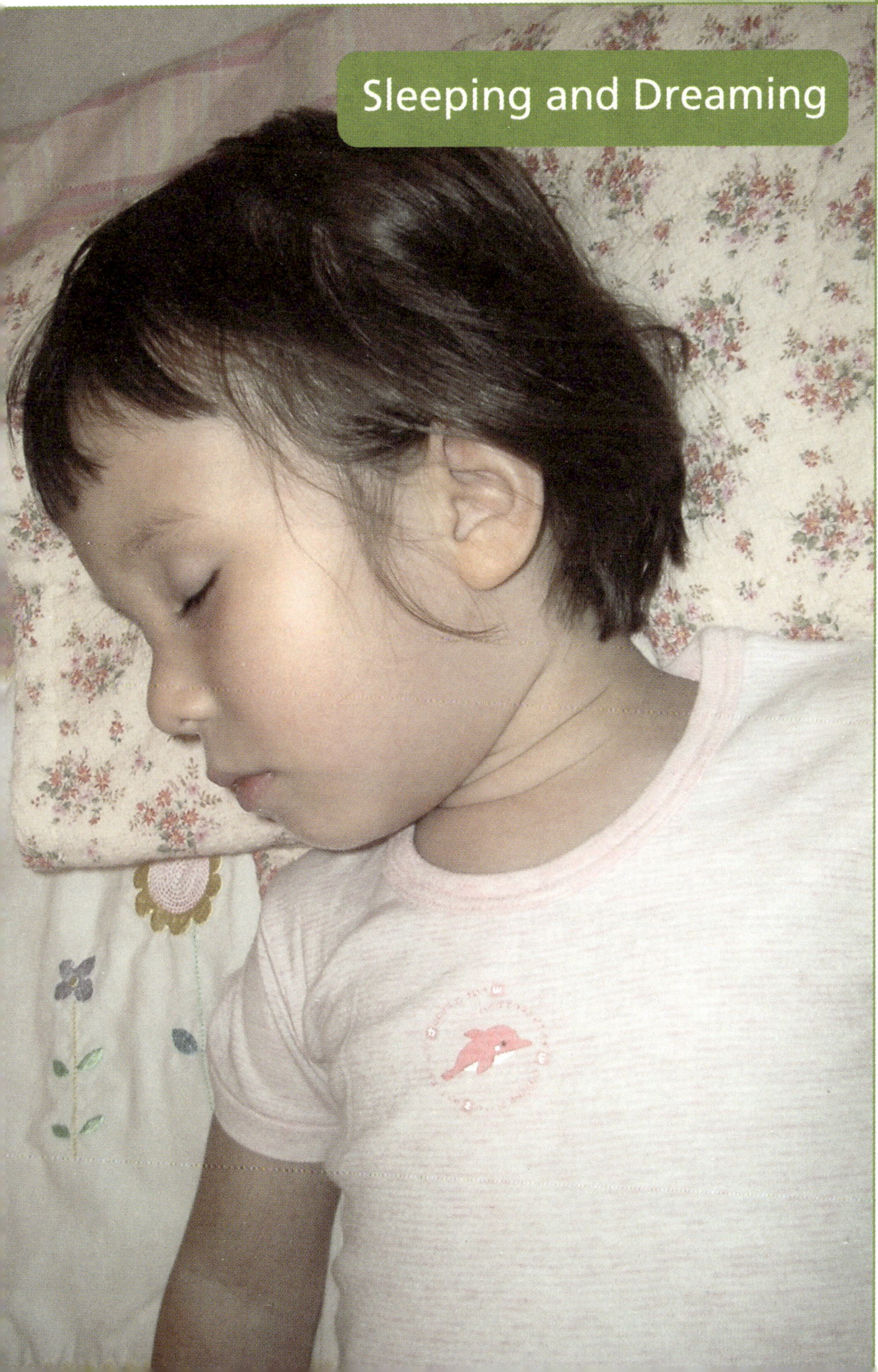

When we use the phrase 'sweet dreams' to send people to bed, we hope that enjoyable dreams will also bring them a good night's sleep. Sleeping and dreaming are very closely connected as it is only during sleep that we dream. Therefore, before we look more closely at dreaming, we need to know a bit about sleep and how the two are related.

We all need sleep

We all need to sleep, even though Thomas Edison (1847–1931), famous inventor of the light bulb, said it was a waste of time. It is easy to understand why he said this because we actually spend about a third of our lives asleep. Imagine all the things we could do if we did not!

Thomas Edison

NOTES

light bulb / laɪt bʌlb / 电灯泡

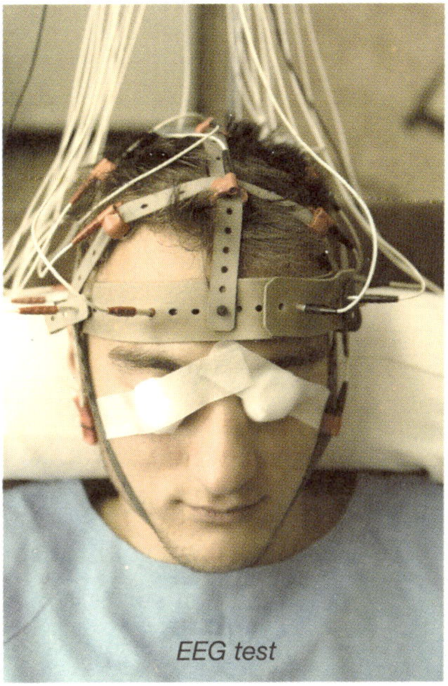
EEG test

For a long time scientists were not interested in studying sleep because they assumed that the brain simply switched off during sleep. However, in 1936, an 'EEG' machine was invented. It could measure brain activity through electrodes placed on a person's head. Scientists suddenly saw that a person's brain was *active* during sleep. Since then, sleep has been studied extensively.

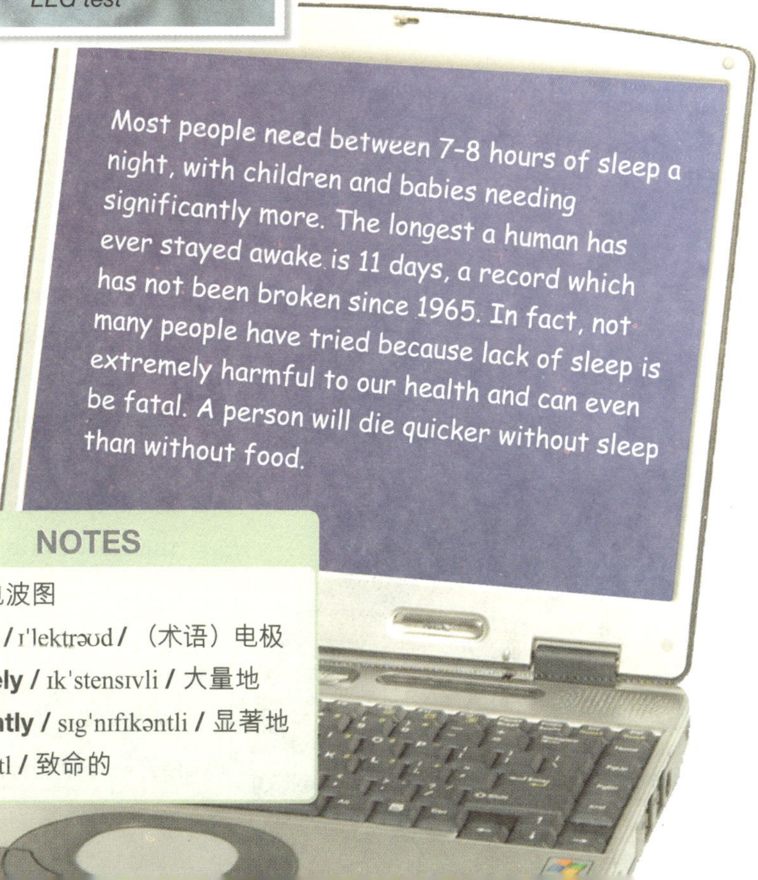

NOTES

EEG 脑电波图
electrode / ɪ'lektrəʊd / （术语）电极
extensively / ɪk'stensɪvli / 大量地
significantly / sɪg'nɪfɪkəntli / 显著地
fatal / 'feɪtl / 致命的

Sleep stages

One of the first things that scientists discovered about our sleeping brains was that we actually have a sleep cycle. They discovered this by studying the lines produced by an EEG that represent brainwaves.

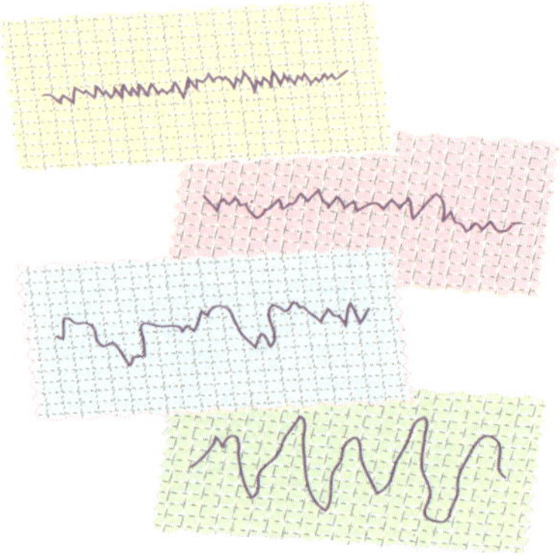

brainwaves

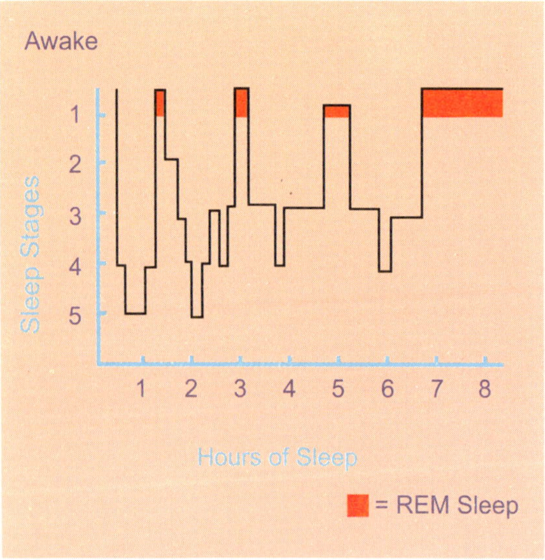

A sleep cycle diagram

During a typical eight-hour sleep, we go through five different stages of sleep about four or five times. In one of these repeated stages, our brains are almost as active as when we are awake. These repeated active stages are called REM sleep, or Rapid Eye Movement sleep. The other four stages of sleep are each marked by a different level of brain activity with stage five, the deepest sleep, showing the least brain activity.

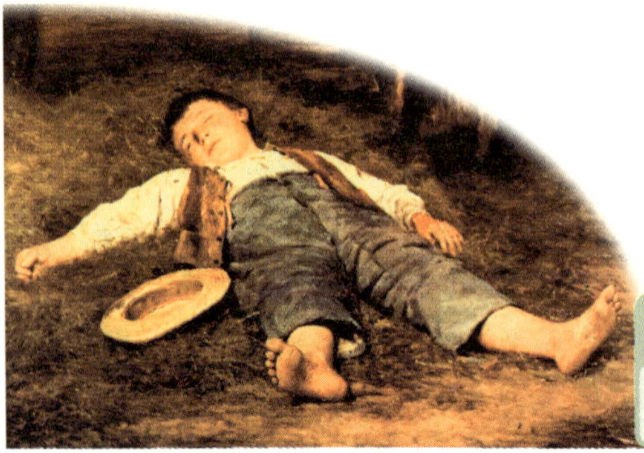

NOTES

cycle / 'saɪkəl / 循环期，周期

So how does dreaming fit into this sleep cycle?

dream *n.* a group of related thoughts, images, or feelings experienced during sleep

REM sleep and dreaming

In 1953, scientists discovered that during the brain's most active period of sleep, the eyes moved very rapidly under the eyelids as if watching things go by. This stage of sleep therefore got the name REM, or Rapid Eye Movement sleep. Scientists also noticed that during REM sleep, breathing and heart rate increased and the body became almost completely paralysed. All these discoveries, along with the heightened brain activity, led them to believe that dreaming must occur during REM sleep. They believed that the body was paralysed to stop people acting out their dreams and hurting themselves.

NOTES

eyelid / ˈaɪlɪd / 眼睑，眼皮

paralysed / ˈpærəlaɪzd / 瘫痪的，麻痹的

heighten / ˈhaɪtn / 加强

Sure enough, when people were woken during REM sleep they usually reported that they had been dreaming. Scientists also found that if people woke up after the REM stage rather than after one of the other sleep stages, they were more likely to remember their dreams.

However, although it seems that most dreaming occurs during REM sleep, recent research has shown that people also dream during other stages, because people who never experience REM sleep (due to brain damage) still report dreaming.

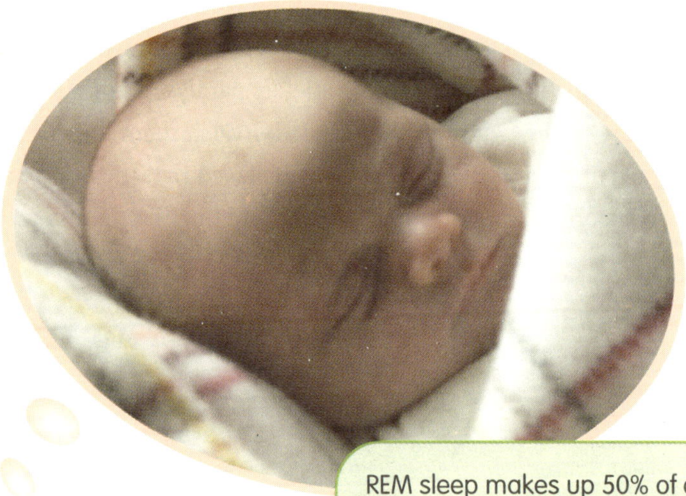

REM sleep makes up 50% of a baby's sleep cycle and only 20% of an adult's. Babies therefore dream more than adults. Research has even detected rapid eye movement in unborn babies from 6 months onwards.

NOTES

detect / dɪ'tekt / 发觉，发现

onwards / 'ɒnwədz / 以后，之后

In the last 50 years, scientists have found out many incredible facts about dreaming.

Believe it or not!

- One cannot dream and snore at the same time.
- Multilingual people dream in different languages depending on the types of dreams.
- Blind people do dream. If they are not born blind, they can see images in their dreams; otherwise they have dreams rich in the other senses.
- Most of a dream is forgotten five minutes after the end of it; after ten minutes, 90% of it is forgotten.
- Men dream more about men while women dream equally about men and women.
- People only start appearing in their own dreams after the age of three or four.

NOTES

incredible / ɪnˈkredɪbəl / 难以置信的

snore / snɔːʳ / 打鼾

multilingual / ˌmʌltɪˈlɪŋgwəl / 多种语言的

How do we dream?

EEGs have enabled scientists to measure brain activity and they have also shown what parts of the brain are active when we dream. Most research has been done on brain activity during REM sleep and it seems that dreams might start with a part of the brain called the pons.

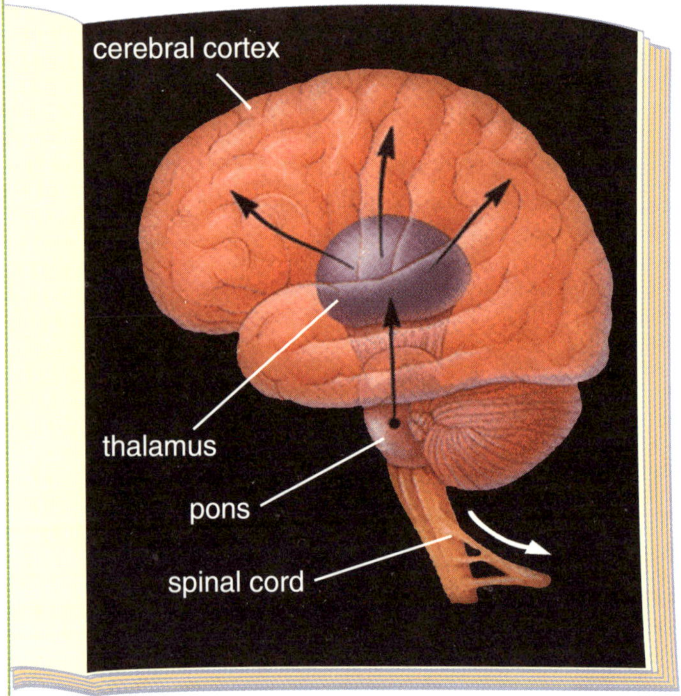

Scientists have found that the pons sends signals to two parts of the brain: the thalamus and the cerebral cortex. The thalamus constantly receives information during the day and sends it on to the cerebral cortex which interprets this information and stores it.

It seems that the signals from the pons stimulate the cerebral cortex to create a stream of images out of all the stored information. People experience these images as dreams.

NOTES

pons / pɒnz / 脑桥
thalamus / 'θæləməs / 丘脑
cerebral cortex / 'serɪbrəl 'kɔ:teks / 大脑皮层
stimulate / 'stɪmjʊleɪt / 刺激

Why do we dream?

We now know when we dream and what happens to our dreaming bodies, but scientists are still not certain about why we dream.

Most dream theories fall into one of two categories: physiological theories and psychological theories. They have distinctly different explanations for the purpose of dreaming.

	Physiological Theories	Psychological Theories
Purpose of dreaming	To help the functioning of our bodies and in particular, our brains.	To deal with our thoughts, emotions and important issues in our lives.

Despite what we've learnt through scientific studies, the land of dreams remains a mysterious place. Read on to find out more about dreams.

NOTES

physiological / ˌfɪziəˈlɒdʒɪkəl / 生理学的
despite / dɪˈspaɪt / 尽管，不管
mysterious / mɪˈstɪəriəs / 神秘的

True or false

Are the following sentences true or false? Circle T for true and F for false.

1. People only dream during REM sleep. T / F
2. EEG machines measure brain activity. T / F
3. Psychological theories of dreaming state that dreams help our brains function. T / F
4. 90% of a dream is forgotten five minutes after the end of it. T / F
5. Scientists do not know exactly why we dream. T / F
6. REM stands for Rapid Eye Machine. T / F
7. It seems that dreams start in the cerebral cortex. T / F
8. Babies dream more than adults. T / F
9. Humans need to sleep. T / F
10. A person can die from lack of sleep. T / F

Answers: 1. F; 2. T; 3. F; 4. F; 5. T; 6. F; 7. F; 8. T; 9. T; 10. T

Types of Dreams

Each dream may seem different, but when you study thousands of them, they begin to fall into certain categories.

Recurring dreams

Many people have the same or a similar dream many times, either over a short period of time or throughout their lives. These dreams usually begin in childhood, and are mostly scenes of being attacked, chased or threatened by wild animals, monsters, people, or natural forces such as storms, fires, or floods.

Scientists say these dreams are associated with unresolved problems in a person's life, or some sort of trauma in the past. Once the trauma has been faced or the problem dealt with, the dream usually goes away.

NOTES

recur / rɪˈkɜːʳ / 一再发生，反复出现
monster / ˈmɒnstəʳ / 怪物，妖怪
unresolved / ˌʌnrɪˈzɒlvd / 未解决的
trauma / ˈtrɔːmə / 精神创伤，痛苦的经历

Nightmares

Nightmares are scary dreams so disturbing that people often wake up feeling anxious and frightened. Unlike other types of dreams, nightmares tend to be remembered for a long time. They are also common among children and people who have had terrible experiences; for example, soldiers who have seen the horror of war or people who have witnessed terrible accidents.

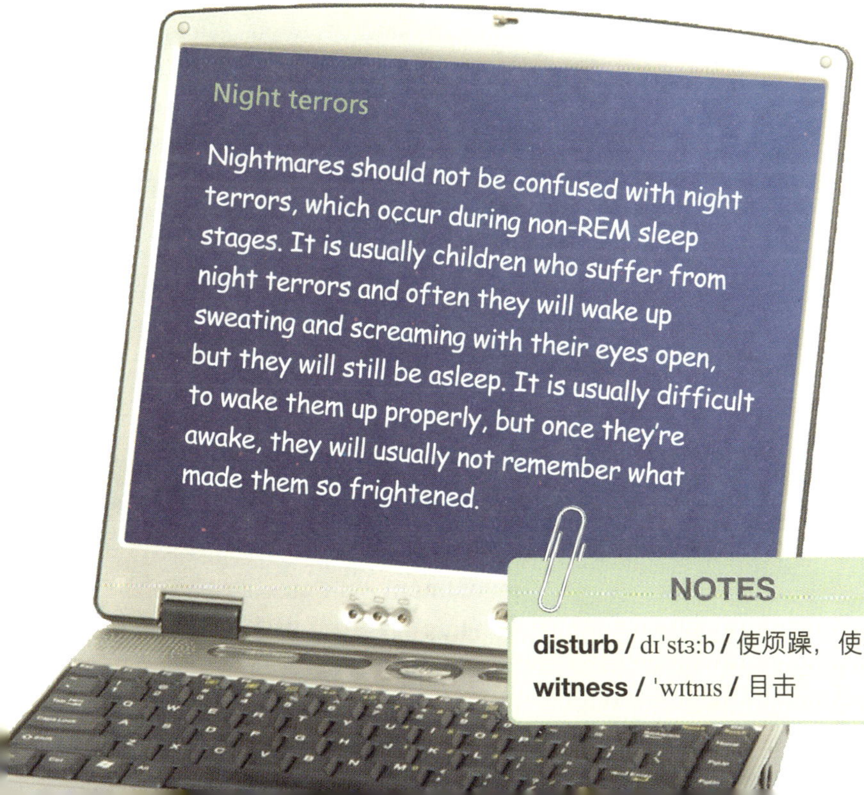

Night terrors

Nightmares should not be confused with night terrors, which occur during non-REM sleep stages. It is usually children who suffer from night terrors and often they will wake up sweating and screaming with their eyes open, but they will still be asleep. It is usually difficult to wake them up properly, but once they're awake, they will usually not remember what made them so frightened.

NOTES

disturb / dɪ'stɜ:b / 使烦躁，使不安

witness / 'wɪtnɪs / 目击

Prophetic dreams

It seems unlikely that people can predict the future in dreams but many people claim to have done so. It is more likely, however, that prophetic dreams are due to coincidence, faulty memory, or an unconscious tying together of known information. Many people have dreams in times of stress and may, for example, dream about a train crash the day before taking a train trip. Of course, trains do crash from time to time and if the train does in fact have an accident, the person who had the dream will tell everyone about it afterwards. If the train does not crash, the dream is likely to be forgotten.

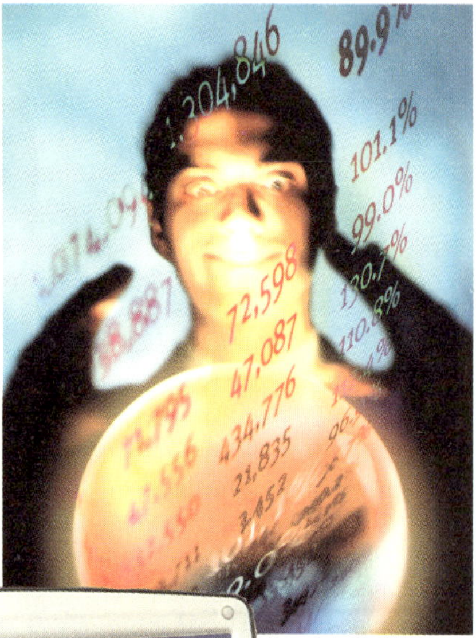

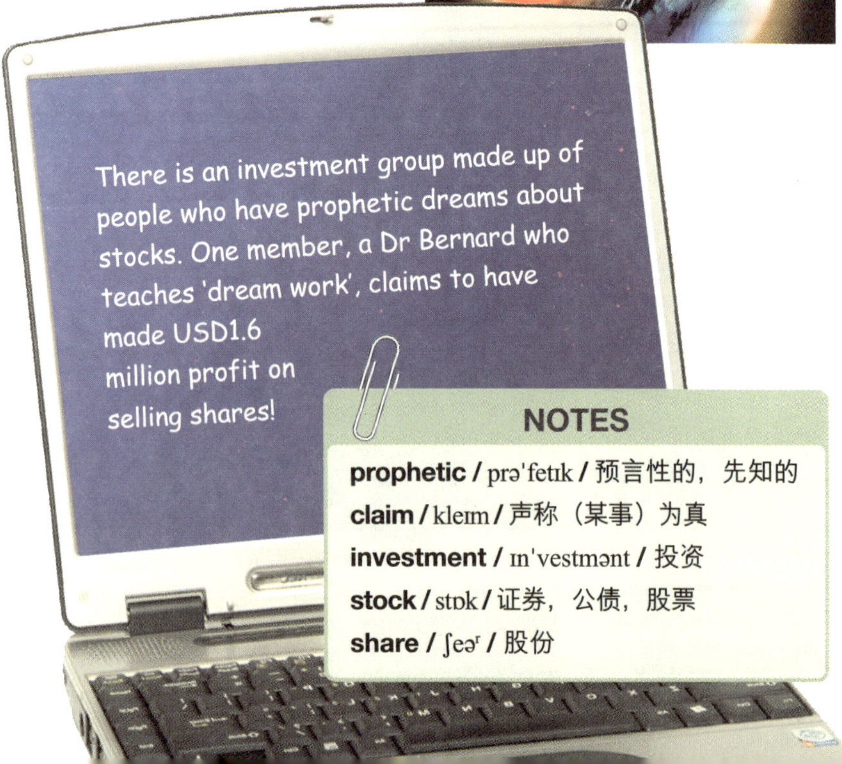

NOTES

prophetic / prə'fetɪk / 预言性的，先知的

claim / kleɪm / 声称（某事）为真

investment / ɪn'vestmənt / 投资

stock / stɒk / 证券，公债，股票

share / ʃeəʳ / 股份

One explanation for prophetic dreams is that during dreams, the mind pieces together ideas and observations that the 'awake' brain absorbed but did not analyse during waking hours.

A good example is a dream the famous psychologist Carl Jung (1875–1961) had in 1914. He dreamt there was a great flood in Europe. The water rose as high as the mountains in Switzerland and thousands of people were drowned. Then the water turned into blood. A few months after this dream occurred, World War I broke out in Europe. Switzerland, a neutral country, was spared.

But was this dream predicting the future, or had Jung actually absorbed a lot of information about European politics when he was awake without realising it? It is easy to give meaning to dreams when you look back.

NOTES

observation / ˌɒbzəˈveɪʃən / 观察，观察到的事物

psychologist / saɪˈkɒlədʒɪst / 心理学家

drown / draʊn / 淹没，溺死

neutral / ˈnju:trəl / 中立的，不偏不倚的

Lucid dreams

Simply speaking, a lucid dream is one that the dreamer knows he is dreaming even though he is still asleep. In such a dream, the dreamer can control events in a variety of interesting ways. With practice, some people can even decide what they will dream about each night.

Lucidity usually begins in the middle of dreams when the dreamers become aware they are dreaming, keeping their own identities and waking memories, yet believing for some reason that, for example, the Eiffel Tower is made of cheese or a lock should be opened with a flower.

NOTES

lucid / ˈluːsɪd / 清醒的

intentionally / ɪnˈtenʃənəli / 有意地，故意地

Lucid dreaming interests many people because they can consciously enjoy what happens in the dream and go on to actively explore the land of dreams. These possibilities have made many people practise lucid dreaming intentionally.

Daydreams

Daydreaming is classified as a level of consciousness between sleep and wakefulness. It occurs during our waking hours when we let our imaginations carry us away. We forget our surroundings and find ourselves in an imagined fantasy world where we are often fulfilling wishes such as winning an Olympic medal. But are daydreams a type of dream, or are they completely different from dreams experienced during sleep?

There are various theories, but the most common view is that daydreams are very different to sleep dreams. It seems that different parts of the brain are used to create sleep dreams and daydreams. While sleep dreams are bizarre, uncertain, and incoherent, daydreams are usually coherent and organised.

Most people daydream sometimes. Some people, however, daydream very easily and they have difficulty concentrating. This can have serious effects on their work.

NOTES

consciousness / ˈkɒnʃəsnɪs / 意识，感觉
fulfil / fʊlˈfɪl / 满足，实现
bizarre / bɪˈzɑːʳ / 奇异的，不寻常的
incoherent / ˌɪnkəʊˈhɪərənt / 不连贯的

Sleepwalking and sleep-talking

Sleepwalking and sleep-talking are not dreams. They are sleeping problems that occur during non-REM sleep when the body is not paralysed. However, a person can be dreaming while they sleepwalk or sleep-talk. This proves again that dreams do not only occur during REM sleep.

About 10% of people sleepwalk at least once in their lives, mostly as children, and both sleepwalking and sleep-talking seem to run in families. Neither of these problems is serious and it is perfectly safe to wake someone up when they are sleepwalking or sleep-talking.

It is not known and is difficult to prove scientifically whether the content of the dream corresponds to the things said or done in sleep.

NOTES

sleepwalking / ˈsli:pˌwɔ:kɪŋ / 梦游

Sleepwalking can sometimes lead to dangerous situations. One American woman had driven her car 20 miles before she woke up at the wheel and realised she had been driving in her sleep.

Sleepwalking can have consequences that are even more serious. In a very controversial court case in England in 2003, a man claimed that he killed his father by mistake while sleepwalking. He was found not guilty of murder but was sent to a mental hospital. Luckily this is an extremely unusual case, but imagine if there was no sleep paralysis during REM sleep. The consequences could be horrific.

NOTES

crane / kreɪn / 起重机，吊车
beam / bi:m / 梁，天平横杆

In London in 2005, a 15-year-old sleepwalker was found fast asleep 40 metres above the ground on a construction crane. She had climbed up the crane and walked across a narrow metal beam while sleeping.

Types of dreams

What types of dreams are these? Check your answers on page 57.

1. ______________________

2. ______________________

3. ______________________

4. ______________________

Interpreting Dreams

Ancient cultural interpretations of dreams

The history of dream interpretation is as long as human history itself. Our ancestors were fascinated, haunted, and alarmed by dreams and, as many of us still do today, they thought that there were messages hidden in dreams. They believed that humans dreamt for a reason, and had various theories to explain what dreams meant.

NOTES

haunt / hɔːnt / 缠扰，缠住，困扰
military / ˈmɪlɪtəri / 军事的

Egypt

In ancient Egypt, dreams were thought to be messages sent from the gods. They could be warnings or predictions of good fortune. People would pray and sleep in the temples of the god of dreams, and priests would interpret their dreams. Priests who could interpret dreams were politically powerful in ancient Egypt.

Greece and Rome

During ancient Greek and Roman times, dream interpreters went to war with military leaders to interpret their dreams and help them make military decisions. In everyday life, particularly unusual dreams were sent to the Roman senate for interpretation.

Babylon

Clay tablets with inscriptions from the area around modern Iraq tell a story about a king's recurring dreams, which were taken as prophecy.

China

For the ancient Chinese, dreams seemed to be actual places where their spirits went at night. They believed that being woken too early could tear the spirit from the body.

America

Some Native American and Mexican people believed that their ancestors lived in their dreams and took on non-human forms like animals or plants. Dreaming was a way to visit their ancestors.

NOTES

inscription / ɪn'skrɪpʃən / 铭刻，碑文

prophecy / 'prɒfɪsi / 预言，预示

A Bible story

The Bible is the most important book in the Christian religion. Christians believe that the Bible is the 'Word of God'. There are more than 700 mentions of dreams in the Bible!

In one story, the Pharaoh of Egypt dreams that seven fat, healthy cows come out of the river Nile, followed by seven thin, sickly cows, which eat the healthy ones. In another dream, seven healthy heads of grain are eaten by seven sickly heads.

When the Jewish prisoner Joseph is called to explain the dreams, he says that seven years of good harvests will be followed by seven years of famine. The Pharaoh believes him and stores enough food to last through the famine.

NOTES

Pharaoh / 'feərəʊ / （古埃及的）法老
Jewish / 'dʒu:ɪʃ / 犹太的
famine / 'fæmɪn / 饥荒

Aristotle and Hippocrates

Aristotle (384 BC–322 BC) was an ancient Greek philosopher who is considered to be one of the most important thinkers in Western history. He was the first person to suggest that dreams are not spiritual or sent by the gods. He believed that dreams are the product of experiences we have while awake, and then used by our imagination during dreaming; or else they arise from internal sensations and can be seen as the symptoms of illness. He thought that dreams could be indicators of the body's condition.

Aristotle

Hippocrates (460 BC–380 BC) was an ancient Greek doctor who is now known as 'the Father of Medicine'. He adopted Aristotle's view and used his patients' dreams to help diagnose their illnesses. However, the spiritual theory still persisted.

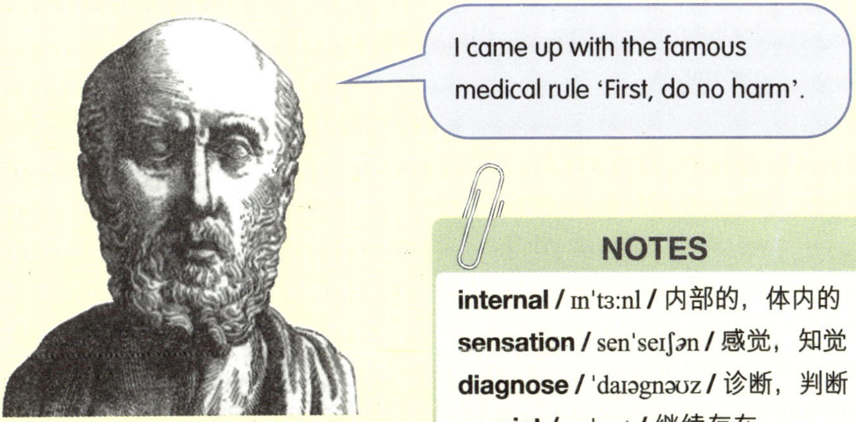

Hippocrates

NOTES

internal / ɪn'tɜ:nl / 内部的，体内的
sensation / sen'seɪʃən / 感觉，知觉
diagnose / 'daɪəgnəʊz / 诊断，判断
persist / pə'sɪst / 继续存在

Modern dream theories

In the early 1800s, a new belief in science began to sweep away attitudes about dreams being part of a spiritual world. Instead, dreams were thought to come from household noises, stress, or poor digestion after dinner. But towards the end of the 19th century, the focus moved from the external world to our internal world.

Sigmund Freud

Sigmund Freud (1856–1939)

Freud was a psychiatrist who is known as 'the father of psychology'. He studied and treated people with mental illnesses, and after years of study, he began to believe that a person's behaviour is not always consciously controlled. Rather, it is often dictated by a force buried deep down in our minds — the unconscious. He used hypnotism and other techniques to gain access to the unconscious of his patients. Finally, in his work *Interpretation of Dreams* published in 1899, he argued that it is during dreams that we visit this largely unexplored part, or level, of our minds.

According to Freud, dreams are about things we unconsciously wish would or would not happen. He called this wish-fulfilment.

NOTES

external / ɪk'stɜ:nəl / 外部的，外在的
psychiatrist / saɪ'kaɪətrɪst / 精神科医生
dictate / dɪk'teɪt / 支配
hypnotism / 'hɪpnətɪzəm / 催眠（术）

Despite his widely accepted theory of the unconscious, psychiatrists do not often agree with Freud's interpretation of the symbols. Many believe that Freud was too focused on relationships between men and women.

Freud believed that what we see in our dreams are symbols that represent the secret wishes in our unconscious minds. These wishes are too outrageous or dark for our conscious minds to believe or accept. In order to prevent them from breaking into our conscious minds, these desires have to be fulfilled in our dreams.

NOTES

outrageous / aʊt'reɪdʒəs /
骇人的，粗暴的

Levels of consciousness

The **conscious** level is the level on which all our thoughts operate, and is responsible for the things we do because we know why we want to do them. Anything that is thought or understood is done on this conscious level.

The **subconscious** level stores memories and thoughts that we may not be aware of all the time, but are ready to enter our conscious level whenever recalled, and may strongly influence our conscious processes.

The **unconscious** level has the wishes, needs, and thoughts that we are completely unaware of, or those that we choose not to be aware of. They threaten to upset us if they break into our conscious minds, so we repress them while awake and entertain them only in our dreams. Freud explained that this is why dreams are often disturbing because we are forced to see what we do not wish to see.

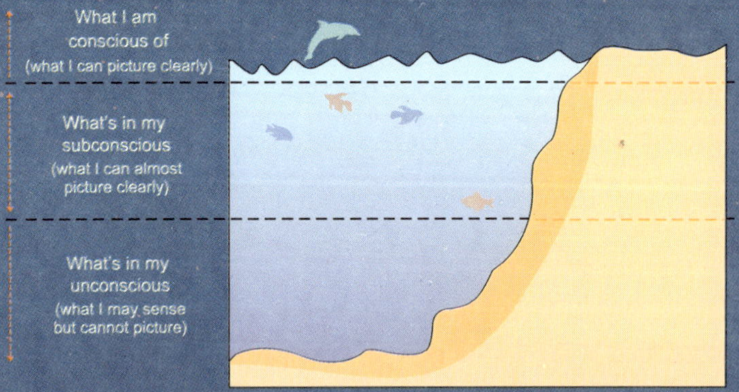

The unconscious is a very important concept in Freud's dream interpretation because he believed that it is where our deepest desires are hidden from our conscious minds.

NOTES

recall / rɪ'kɔ:l / 回想

repress / rɪ'pres / 抑制，压制

Carl Jung (1875–1961)

Carl Jung

At first, Jung was a follower of Freud, but later he developed his own theory. He believed that dreams are not trying to hide anything from us; instead, they are trying to reveal things to us. Therefore, in order to understand ourselves better and lead happy lives, our conscious minds have to be aware of, and 'reconcile with', our unconscious minds. The best way to do this is to analyse our dreams.

Jung's study of dreams led him to believe that symbols are used to represent ideas that we cannot understand (compared to ideas we cannot accept as claimed by Freud) during the day. He believed that through our dreams, we analyse these symbols and come to understand the ideas they represent.

NOTES

reveal / rɪ'viːl / 暴露，揭示

reconcile / 'rekənsaɪl / 调解，调和

Real dreams

Zhuang Zi was a Chinese philosopher who lived sometime in the 4th century BC. He once had a dream that he was a butterfly. When he woke up, he no longer knew if he was a butterfly dreaming he was a man, or a man who had dreamed he was a butterfly!

Write down a dream you have had that felt so real when you woke up that you believed it was true for a while.

Common and Famous Dreams

Common dreams

Believe it or not, despite wide differences between cultures and individuals, people around the world often have similar dreams. There are a few themes that are particularly common.

Being chased

Chase dreams are very common and are often frightening. They can represent a person's fear of being attacked, but usually they reflect how we are dealing with anxiety and problems in our waking lives — by running away from them rather than facing them.

Psychologists suggest that if we know what is chasing us, we may discover the source of our fears and will be able to overcome them.

NOTES

individual / ˌɪndɪˈvɪdʒʊəl **/** 个人，个体

Flying

Most flying dreams are lucid dreams which mean they can be controlled. They are usually exciting and leave dreamers with a great sense of freedom.

If you fly with ease, then it suggests that you are on top of a situation in your waking life. You have risen above something. Having difficulties flying indicates a lack of power in controlling a certain situation. You might struggle to fly above a tree or a mountain. These are symbols that represent a particular obstacle or person who is standing in your way in your waking life. If you feel fear when flying or feel that you are flying too high, then it suggests that you are afraid of challenges and of success.

However, some scientists claim that flying dreams might mean nothing. They might simply be caused by a consciousness of motion during sleep, for example, when the dreamer is sleeping on a train.

Studies show that musicians, artists, and public speakers are more likely to have flying dreams.

NOTES

obstacle / ˈɒbstəkəl / 障碍，妨碍

motion / ˈməʊʃən / 运动，移动

Failing an exam

Have you ever dreamt about failing an exam because the time runs out or you can't find your pen? Don't worry — they are not prophetic dreams; they're only a measure of your self-esteem and confidence. Psychologists say that people who worry about not being good enough are likely to have such dreams. These dreams may also be related to guilt about not working hard enough. The good news is that people who have this kind of dream rarely fail in real life.

Falling

As with most common dream themes, falling is a sign of insecurity. You are feeling out of control in some situations in your waking life, possibly in a relationship or at school. Falling dreams usually occur during the first stage of sleep and are often accompanied by muscle spasms of the arms and legs which can wake the dreamer.

NOTES

self-esteem / ˌselfɪˈstiːm / 自尊

insecurity / ˌɪnsɪˈkjʊərɪti / 担忧，不安全

spasm / ˈspæzəm / 痉挛，抽筋

Being naked in public

Dreaming that you are naked in public is very common and can symbolise a lot of things. It could mean that you are hiding something and are afraid that others can see right through you. It could also mean that you are pretending to be something you are not in your waking life, or that you are scared of being laughed at. Being naked also symbolises being caught off guard. Perhaps you are not prepared for a project at school or work.

Losing teeth

Dreams in which your teeth crumble or fall out one by one can be horrifying and shocking. But what do they mean? One theory is that these dreams reflect your worry about your appearance. Another theory is that since teeth are used for biting and chewing, loss of teeth might represent a feeling of powerlessness in a situation in your waking life.

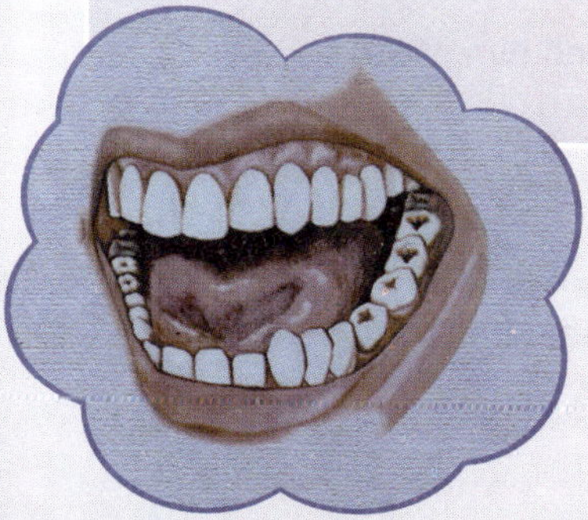

NOTES

naked / ˈneɪkɪd / 裸体的，赤裸的
symbolise / ˈsɪmbəlaɪz / 象征，代表
off guard 处于松懈状态
crumble / ˈkrʌmbəl / 碎裂

Famous dreams

Many famous people have had dreams that they claimed were prophetic like Carl Jung's dream of the flood in Europe. Some have even claimed that their famous inventions, ideas or books were inspired by dreams. These dreams have become very well-known.

Read on and decide for yourself whether these famous dreams were really meaningful or if the famous dreamers were simply letting their imaginations run away with them.

Abraham Lincoln predicting his own death

Abraham Lincoln

American President Abraham Lincoln (1809–1865) was assassinated in 1865. He was shot in the back of the head while watching a play at the theatre. A short while before the assassination, Lincoln told several friends about a dream that had disturbed him greatly. After the event, his friends remembered the dream. The dream seemed to have accurately predicted that he was soon to die.

NOTES

assassinate / ə'sæsɪneɪt / 暗杀，行刺

I began to dream. I thought I left my bed and wandered downstairs. There the silence was broken by pitiful sobbing, but the mourners were invisible. I went from room to room; no living person was in sight. I kept on until I arrived at the East Room, which I entered. There I met with a sickening surprise. Before me rested a corpse. Around it were stationed soldiers. 'Who is dead in the White House?' I demanded of one of the soldiers. 'The President' was his answer. 'He was killed by an assassin!'

It is not surprising that Lincoln had such a dream. America had just experienced a great civil war and many people were opposed to Lincoln and had reason to kill him. Lincoln was a brave man, but his fears may have conquered his dreams.

NOTES

invisible / ɪnˈvɪzɪbəl / 看不见的，无形的

corpse / kɔːps / 尸体

conquer / ˈkɒŋkəʳ / 击败，征服

Albert Einstein

An inspirational dream

Many scientists claim to have dreamt up solutions to problems they have been studying. Even Albert Einstein (1879–1955), the most famous scientist of the 20th century, once said that his 1905 paper on the theory of relativity was inspired by a dream.

In his dream, he sped down a mountainside on a sled. As he approached the speed of light, the stars began to change.

In 1905, Einstein was working as a clerk in Switzerland, struggling to make enough money to support his new wife. This period of his life is described in a 1994 novel called *Einstein's Dreams*, which supposes that Einstein's theories on time were all based on his dreams.

NOTES

inspirational / ˌɪnspɪˈreɪʃənəl / 激发灵感的

theory of relativity 相对论

Changing history

What would have happened if Adolf Hitler (1889–1945) had been killed during World War I (1914–1918)? If Hitler had not had a dream one night that saved his life, World War II would probably never have happened and the history of the 20th century would have been completely different.

Adolf Hitler

During WWI, Hitler was asleep in a trench when he dreamt that he and the other soldiers with him were buried in earth and metal. He woke up and left the trench to go for a walk. While he was away, the trench was hit by a bomb and all the other soldiers were killed.

NOTES

trench / trentʃ / 沟，渠，壕

A famous book

Frankenstein is a famous science fiction book which tells of a scientist who builds a monster out of human body parts and brings it to life. In 1831, the author, Mary Shelley (1797–1851), told people that the story was inspired by a nightmare she had after a night reading ghost stories with friends. But some people suggest that the novel might also be inspired by another dream, in which she saw her own dead child.

I saw the hideous phantasm of a man stretched out, and then, on the working of some powerful engine, show signs of life, and stir with an uneasy, half-vital motion.

I dreamt that my little baby came to life again, that it had only been cold, and that we rubbed it before the fire, and it lived.

Mary Shelley

NOTES

Frankenstein / ˈfræŋkɪnstaɪn / 弗兰肯斯泰因（一个创造怪物而自己被他毁灭的医学研究者）
hideous / ˈhɪdiəs / 极其丑陋的，令人惊骇的
phantasm / ˈfæntæzəm / 幻像，幽灵

The first woman millionaire

Madam C. J. Walker (1867–1919) is famous for becoming the first woman to earn a million dollars. She was a poor labourer who lost her hair from illness in the 1890s. Claiming that it was shown to her in a dream, she created a hair treatment that went on to make her rich.

Madam C. J. Walker

Dr Frederick Banting

A cure

Dr Frederick Banting (1891–1941) wanted to find a cure for diabetes — the disease that had killed his mother. The answer came to him in a dream and it won him the Nobel Prize for Medicine in 1923.

The invention of the sewing machine

In 1845, Elias Howe (1819–1867) had a dream that helped him invent the sewing machine. He dreamt that he was in Africa and that cannibals had put him in a pot of boiling water. He tried to get out but they pushed him back in with their spears. When he woke, terrified, he realised that each spear had a hole in its tip, just like a long sewing needle.

Elias Howe

NOTES

diabetes / ˌdaɪəˈbiːtiːz / 糖尿病
cannibal / ˈkænɪbəl / 食人族
spear / spɪəʳ / 长矛

People and their dreams

Read about these people and decide what common dreams they might have.

a) Flying
b) Losing teeth
c) Failing an exam
d) Naked in an inappropriate place

1. Mary is very worried about what she looks like. She wants other people to think she is pretty.

2. Yuki has told everyone at school that his family is rich. He is worried that they'll find out he is lying.

3. Treena is writing an important exam next week. She feels guilty that she went shopping on the weekend instead of studying.

4. Amanda has just won a scholarship to study abroad. She had to work hard to win it but now has a great career ahead of her.

Answers: 1. b); 2. d); 3. c); 4. a)

Study Your Own Dreams

Many people are disturbed by what they dream. They feel uncomfortable in the morning because they wake up confused about what their dreams mean. Studying your own dreams can help you to understand them better, and perhaps even understand yourself better too.

Keeping a dream diary

Dream interpretation is impossible if you cannot remember your dreams. Dreams are forgotten extremely quickly once you wake up, so if you want to start remembering and interpreting them, the best thing to do is to keep a dream diary.

STEP 1

Before falling asleep, say the following to yourself several times:

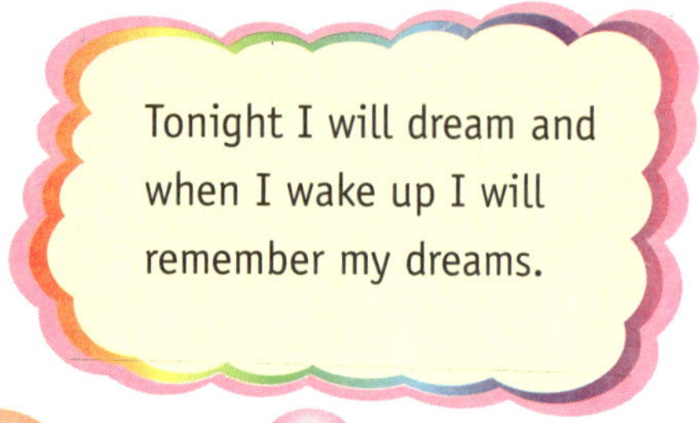

STEP 2

When you wake up, do not open your eyes immediately. Try to think about what you have been dreaming. With practice, you will remember more and more of your dreams.

STEP 3

Keep a notebook and pen beside your bed and write down anything that comes to mind when you wake up — even in the middle of the night. You don't have to write down all the details, just enough clues so that you can recall the dream later. Other than words, you can also draw quick sketches of anything you saw.

NOTES

clue / klu: / 线索，提示

sketch / sketʃ / 草图，速写

Analysing your own dreams

Freud and Jung told us something about analysing our dreams. Freud thought that everything in a dream is a symbol that represents something else, but Jung further developed this idea and thought that the meanings of some symbols are universal.

SYMBOLS IN DREAMS

Bird	Thoughts, so a flying bird means moving and changing thoughts. It is also associated with freedom.
Box	Mystery, secrecy, and precious things. It is also related to the female body.
Ferry	To dream of riding a ferry means going through some transitional phases in life. It also means setting new goals.
Hotel	It may reflect the need for rest and reflection, or a new identity.
Elephant	Power, strength, and intelligence. It also means a lack of patience towards others.

NOTES

mystery / 'mɪstəri / 神秘的事物
transitional / træn'zɪʃənəl / 转变的，过渡的
phase / feɪz / 阶段，时期

Only you know how you feel about certain things or what your real hopes and fears are, so try to interpret your dreams by studying them in relation to your own unique situation.

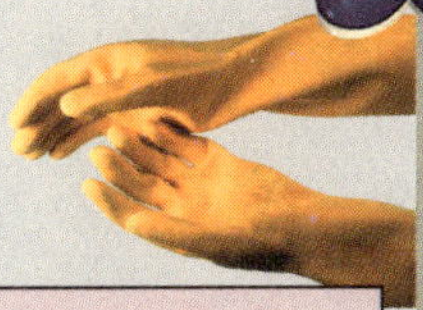

Gloves	Protection, comfort and warmth. They may also symbolise being out of touch with some important things or people.
Door, Gate	Going through a door may mean moving on to a different period of your life. Locked doors may represent obstacles.
Jungle	Confusing daily thoughts. It also reflects worry about a particular situation or difficulty.
King	Powerful people like a father, teacher, boss etc. It also signifies success.
Umbrella	An object the conscious mind uses to protect itself from the unconscious. Some interpretations say that it is a symbol of security.

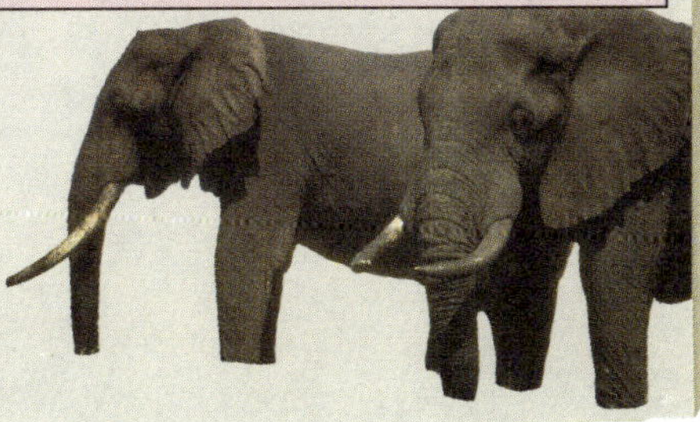

NOTES

signify / ˈsɪgnɪfaɪ /
意味着，表示

You may try to find meanings in your dreams, particularly if they trouble you. But remember that even the top scientists today still do not know why we dream, let alone what our dreams really mean. The land of dreams is a fascinating place, but the waking world is where we make our dreams come true. As a wise person once said,

'Some people dream of success... while others wake up and work hard at it.'

Interpret this dream

Last night Tim had this dream. Using Jung's symbols, what do you think it might mean?

'I was walking in a jungle and couldn't find the way out. I could see people I knew amongst the trees but I couldn't touch them and they couldn't see me. Suddenly, a king was walking towards me. He held an umbrella over my head and he led me towards a door. It was locked. We stopped at the door and the king disappeared. I looked at my hands and saw that I was wearing gloves. I took them off and there in my hand was a key! I opened the door and on the other side was an elephant surrounded by all the people I knew looking at me and smiling.'

Understanding topics of paragraphs
理解段落的主题

When you read a text, read each paragraph carefully and underline 3–5 of the most important words. Be careful, the first sentence in a paragraph often introduces the main idea, but not always!
看一篇文章时应仔细地阅读每个段落，并找出三至五个关键词，在其下划线。要留意的是，每一段的第一个句子通常说明该段的中心，但也有例外。

Practice 练习

Read the following three paragraphs carefully and match them with their topics.
仔细阅读下面三段文字，然后将每段与其主题配对。

a) conscious level b) subconscious level c) unconscious level

1

This level has the wishes, needs, and thoughts that we are completely unaware of, or those that we choose not to be aware of. They threaten to upset us if they break into our conscious minds, so we repress them while awake and entertain them only in our dreams. Freud explained that this is why dreams are often disturbing.

2

This level stores memories and thoughts that we may not be aware of all the time, but are ready to enter our conscious level whenever recalled, and may strongly influence our conscious processes.

3

This is the level on which all of our thoughts operate, and is responsible for the things we do because we know why we want to do them. Anything that is thought or understood is on this conscious level.

Do you know?

- It is the brain's most active period of sleep.
- To stop us acting out our dreams and hurting ourselves.
- No. Babies dream more than adults.
- Yes.
- It is a dream that the dreamer knows he is dreaming even though he is still asleep.
- He adopted Aristotle's view and used his patients' dreams to help diagnose their illnesses.
- It can mean that a person is afraid of being attacked.
- They represent power, strength, and intelligence. They may also mean a lack of patience towards others.

Activity

Page 26

1. recurring dreams
2. nightmares
3. lucid dreams
4. prophetic dreams

Page 55

It might mean that Tim was worrying about a particular situation or difficulty in his waking life. There was a powerful person who tried to help him, but they encountered some obstacles. Tim was then alone and out of touch with some important things or people. Finally Tim overcame the obstacles and regained his power, strength and intelligence.

Reading Skills

Page 56

1. c 2. b 3. a

上海外语教育出版社　中学英语分级阅读
Longman 朗文　新课标百科丛书《说梦》
SFLEP–Longman Secondary English Graded Readers
Dreams

This simplified Chinese characters edition first published
in 2006 jointly by Shanghai Foreign Language Education Press
and Pearson Education Asia Ltd.

上海外语教育出版社
培生教育出版亚洲有限公司　联合出版